The Animal After Whom Other Animals Are Named

SERIES EDITORS

Chris Abani

John Alba Cutler

Reginald Gibbons

Susannah Young-ah Gottlieb

Ed Roberson

The Animal After Whom Other Animals Are Named

Poems

Nicole Sealey

NORTHWESTERN UNIVERSITY PRESS

EVANSTON, ILLINOIS

Northwestern University Press
www.nupress.northwestern.edu

Northwestern University Poetry and Poetics Colloquium
poetry.northwestern.edu

Printed in the United States of America

10 9 8 7 6 5 4 3 2 1

Library of Congress Cataloging-in-Publication Data

Sealey, Nicole, author.
   The animal after whom other animals are named : poems / Nicole Sealey.
      pages cm — (Drinking gourd chapbook poetry prize)
   ISBN 978-0-8101-3312-9 (pbk. : alk. paper)
   I. Title. II. Series: Drinking gourd chapbook poetry prize.
PS3619.E25515A84 2016
811.6—dc23

                                                      2015031418

Contents

Foreword by Chris Abani   *vii*

Acknowledgments   *ix*

The First Person Who Will Live to Be One Hundred and
    Fifty Years Old Has Already Been Born   *1*

Medical History   *2*

Instead of Executions, Think Death Erections   *3*

Candelabra with Heads   *4*

Virginia is for Lovers   *5*

Unframed   *6*

Object Permanence   *7*

Legendary   *8*

And   *9*

Clue   *11*

Clue   *14*

Imagine Sisyphus Happy   *17*

Even the Gods   *19*

Legendary   *20*

In Igboland   *21*

Notes   *23*

Foreword

Chris Abani

The poems in this chapbook are insistent yet ephemeral, with pulsing lines that are at once robust and vulnerable, fiercely political and bashfully private. Nicole Sealey has described her work as "an obsession with the declination of the body, a running theme I've been unable to escape." I agree with her idea that the body is often the site of the conversation in these poems and, while there is declination clearly at work (both in the sense of shifts in the magnetic axes and as a kind of refusal), there is also the way in which, while leaning into the private self of the body—a lyric inclination of the American poet—here the body also appears as the site of the political, of the state.

This posture brings to mind the way the poet Sappho used the lyric (or invented the form, as some have asserted) both as a place for the small "self" to enter the conversation normally left only to the epic, but also as a site of resistance to the pressures of state and epic. "Medical History," which is one of the opening poems, finds a delicate balance between what constitutes intimacy and what constitutes information (at once the idea of small self and public self) with the lines:

> I've been pregnant. I've had sex with a man
> who's had sex with men. I can't sleep.

What is startling here is that it is the phrase "I can't sleep" that creates intimacy and breaks the spell of distance. It is both unexpected and so small—and it achieves the turn with such deftness and risk—that it reminds one of the small but powerful turn in William Carlos Williams's "The Red Wheelbarrow." And because the content of the poem is intimate while unashamedly political, it asserts its political sensibility without rebellion but with a confidence that becomes compelling.

In the wonderfully titled "Instead of Executions, Think Death Erections," we see Sealey's satirical skills on display. Hers is not a mocking satire; it is a fragile one that mocks not people but the human condition, and in this way implicates the poet:

> . . . show me
> one pretty thing no heavier
> than a hummingbird.

This is followed by "Candelabra with Heads," a poem about the devastation of lynching and the silence still surrounding that part of our history. It highlights the way in which art is both the only vehicle and yet a weak vehicle for breaking this silence. Like Billie Holiday's "Strange Fruit," it is the phrasing (both of words and music) that dissolves the page, making the experience of the reader visceral.

Poems such as "Unframed" and "Object Permanence" reveal a soft and romantic yet never sentimental side, striving for that language that eludes all poets—the true love poem. The deep chord these poems strike, one of melancholic yearning, indicates how well Sealey achieves this.

"Clue" displays the playful vitality of this collection, with the poem revealing and hiding itself, form echoing content and exhibiting the beginnings of a flirtation with the avant-garde.

In the end this is a collection that enacts what I consider to be the true power of poetry—that a poem is a code, a rogue computer virus, a simulacrum all at once, and that it performs a gentle act of revolution not only against singular meaning, but against the reader's and even the poet's attempts to control and deploy it in singular ways. In this way the poem lives in the world independently and remakes the terrains of meaning and lyric depending on what a reader brings to it. It is both a mirror and a window into the ineffable.

And so I urge you to read Nicole Sealey's work and see it as a condensed manifesto for the larger canvas of fragility, political satire, and love that will emerge from her as her career grows and she adds more books to her résumé.

Acknowledgments

This book is for my sisters: Vanessa Phillips, Sophia Martin, and Renee Kydd.

I would like to extend my deepest gratitude to my husband and parents for their unwavering support. My sincere appreciation to Jericho Brown, Martha Collins, Kimiko Hahn, Linda Susan Jackson, Major Jackson, Naomi Jackson, Yusef Komunyakaa, Deborah Landau, Rickey Laurentiis, Alison Meyers, Marilyn Nelson, and Sharon Olds for their invaluable counsel. Thanks also to the following institutions, without which I would not have had the resources to complete this work: Atlantic Center for the Arts, Cave Canem Foundation, Community of Writers at Squaw Valley, Elizabeth George Foundation, Fine Arts Work Center in Provincetown, Hedgebrook, and New York University's Graduate Creative Writing Program.

Endless appreciation for Poetry and Poetics at Northwestern University and the judges of the 2015 Drinking Gourd Chapbook Poetry Prize—Chris Abani, John Alba Cutler, Reginald Gibbons, Susannah Gottlieb, and Ed Roberson. Thank you for this honor.

Finally, grateful acknowledgment to the editors of the publications in which poems from this chapbook first appeared: *The Account, The American Poetry Review, Copper Nickel, Day One, The New Sound, Ploughshares, Poetry International, Stonecutter, Third Coast, Tupelo Quarterly*, and *The Village Voice*.

The First Person Who Will Live to Be One Hundred and Fifty Years Old Has Already Been Born

For Petra

Scientists say the average human
life gets three months longer every year.
By this math, death will be optional. Like a tie
or dessert or suffering. My mother asks
whether I'd want to live forever.
"I'd get bored," I tell her. "But," she says,
"there's so much to do," meaning
she believes there's much she hasn't done.
Thirty years ago she was the age I am now
but, unlike me, too industrious to think about
birds disappeared by rain. If only we had more
time or enough money to be kept on ice
until such a time science could bring us back.
Of late my mother has begun to think life
short-lived. I'm too young to convince her
otherwise. The one and only occasion
I was in the same room as the *Mona Lisa*,
it was encased in glass behind what I imagine
were velvet ropes. There's far less between
ourselves and oblivion—skin that often defeats
its very purpose. Or maybe its purpose
isn't protection at all, but rather to provide
a place, similar to a doctor's waiting room,
in which to sit until our names are called.
Hold your questions until the end.
Mother, measure my wide-open arms—
we still have *this much* time to kill.

Medical History

I've been pregnant. I've had sex with a man
who's had sex with men. I can't sleep.
My mother has, my mother's mother had,
asthma. My father had a stroke. My father's
mother has high blood pressure.
Both grandfathers died from diabetes.
I drink. I don't smoke. Xanax for flying.
Propranolol for anxiety. My eyes are bad.
I'm spooked by wind. Cousin Lilly died
from an aneurysm. Aunt Hilda, a heart attack.
Uncle Ken, wise as he was, was hit
by a car as if to disprove whatever theory
toward which I write. And, I understand,
the stars in the sky are already dead.

Instead of Executions, Think Death Erections

I wish the day hadn't.
Dawn has claimed
another sky, its birds.

I watch from my burning
stake the broken necks.
Once, this lot

allowed wildflowers,
nothing worse than bruised
wildflowers. Darling

dawn, death mask
to which I've grown
accustomed, show me

one pretty thing
no heavier
than a hummingbird.

Candelabra with Heads

After the sculpture by Thomas Hirschhorn

Had I not brought with me my mind
as it has been made, this thing,
this brood of mannequins, cocooned
and mounted on a wooden scaffold,
might be eight infants swaddled and sleeping.
Might be eight fleshy fingers on one hand.
Might be a family tree with eight pictured
frames. Such treaties occur in the brain.

Can you see them hanging? Their shadow
is a crowd stripping the tree of souvenirs.
Skin shrinks and splits. The bodies weep
fat the color of yolk. Can you smell the burning?

fat the color of yolk. Can you smell the burning?
Skin shrinks and splits. The bodies weep
is a crowd stripping the tree of souvenirs.
Can you see them hanging? Their shadow

frames. Such treaties occur in the brain.
Might be a family tree with eight pictured
Might be eight fleshy fingers on one hand.
might be eight infants swaddled and sleeping.
and mounted on a wooden scaffold,
this brood of mannequins, cocooned
as it has been made, this thing,
Had I not brought with me my mind

Virginia is for Lovers

At LaToya's Pride picnic,
Leonard tells me he and his longtime
love, Pete, broke up.
He says Pete gave him the *house
in Virginia*. "Great," I say,
"that's the least his ass could do."
I daydream my friend and me
into his new house, sit us in the kitchen
of his three-bedroom, two-bath
brick colonial outside Hungry Mother Park,
where, legend has it, the Shawnee raided
settlements with the wherewithal
of wild children catching pigeons.
A woman and her androgynous child
escaped, wandering the wilderness,
stuffing their mouths with the bark
of chokecherry root.
Such was the circumstance
under which the woman collapsed.
The child, who could say nothing
except *hungry mother*, led help
to the mountain where the woman lay,
swelling as wood swells in humid air.
Leonard's mouth is moving.
Two boys hit a shuttlecock back and forth
across an invisible net.
A toddler struggles to pull her wagon
from a sandbox. "No," Leonard says,
"It's not a place where you live.
I got the *H In V. H I*—"
Before my friend could finish,
and as if he'd been newly ordained,
I took his hands and kissed them.

Unframed

Handle this body. Spoil
it with oils. Let the
residue corrode, ruin it.
I have no finish, no
fragile edge. (On what
scrap of me have we
not made desire paths,
so tried as to bury
ourselves therein?) I
beg: spare me gloved
hands, monuments to
nothing. I mean to die a
relief against every wall.

Object Permanence

For John

We wake as if surprised the other is still there,
each petting the sheet to be sure.

How have we managed our way
to this bed—beholden to heat like dawn

indebted to light. Though we're not so self-
important as to think everything

has led to this, everything has led to this.
There's a name for the animal

love makes of us—named, I think,
like rain, for the sound it makes.

You are the animal after whom other animals
are named. Until there's none left to laugh,

days will start with the same startle
and end with caterpillars gorged on milkweed.

O, how we entertain the angels
with our brief animation. O,

how I'll miss you when we're dead.

Legendary

I'd like to be a spoiled rich white girl.

—VENUS XTRAVAGANZA

I want to be married in church. In white.
Nothing borrowed or blue. I want a white
house in Peekskill, far from the city—white
picket fence fencing in my lily-white
lilies. O, were I whiter than white.
A couple kids: one girl, one boy. Both white.
Birthright. All the amenities of white:
golf courses, guesthouses, garage with white
washer/dryer set. Whatever else white
affords, I want. In multiples of white.
Two of nothing is something, if they're white.
Never mind another neutral. Off-white
won't do. Capeesh? I want to be white
as the unsparing light at tunnel's end.

And

After Thomas Sayers Ellis

Withstand pandemonium
and scandalous
nightstands
commanding candlelight

     and
     quicksand

and zinfandel
clandestine landmines
candy handfuls
and contraband

     and
     handmade

commandments
and merchandise
secondhand husbands
philandering

     and
     landless

and vandal
bandwagons slandered
and branded
handwritten reprimands

and
meander

on an island
landscaped with chandeliers
abandon handcuffs
standstills

and
backhands

notwithstanding
thousands of oleanders
and dandelions
handpicked

and
sandalwood

and mandrake
and random demands
the bystander
wanders

in
wonderland.

Clue

After the board game

i

"Hands down, mustard
is the tastiest condiment," coughed Professor Plum—
his full mouth feigning hunger for the greens-
only sandwiches Mrs. White
laid out for Mr. Boddy's guests. Miss Scarlet
hadn't time to peel off her peacoat

before the no-frills food, which she declined, and a pre-cocktail
cocktail, which she accepted. Colonel Mustard
refused all fare, citing the risk of sullying his scarlet
and gold Marine Corps suit, then ate the sugarplums
that happenchanced his pockets like lint. Mrs. White
funneled the motley crew into the green-

house, where Mr. Green
was rumoring—his hand bridging his mouth to Mrs. Peacock's
ear in an effort to convince the white-
haired heiress that the sandwich-making maidservant must've
poisoned their plum
wine. Mr. Boddy's award-winning scarlet

runners initially amused Miss Scarlet,
the way one is amused by another with the same name. Mr. Green
thought it odd Mr. Boddy didn't show, told Professor Plum
as much. "Here we are, pretty as peacocks,
and our host is nowhere to be found," twirling his mustache
like the villain in a silent black and white.

Minutes into the conservatory tour, Mrs. White
introduced Mr. Boddy, who lay facedown in a scarlet-
berried elder. "This man," Colonel Mustard
said, "is dead. I know death, even when it's camouflaged by greenery."
The discovery proved too much for Mrs. Peacock's
usual aplomb—

she fainted into the arms of Professor Plum.
When she came to, he appeared to her the way a white
knight would look to a distressed damsel. Semiconscious, Mrs. Peacock
pointed to the deceased's pet Scarlet
Tanager perched on a lead pipe between the body and a briefcase gushing
    green-
backs. Right away, Colonel Mustard

mustered up an alibi about admiring Mr. Boddy's plumerias.
Mr. Green followed suit with his own white-
washed version involving one Miss Scarlet and a misdemeanor plea
    copped . . .

ii
"Dinner is served," said Mrs. White,
inviting Mr. Boddy's guests by their *noms de plume*
into the dining room for a precooked
reheated repast. Miss Scarlet
passed the pickings, which didn't pass muster,
to a rather ravenous Mr. Green.

Nobody faked affability better than Mr. Green,
waving his napkin like a white
flag, acting out the conquered in Colonel Mustard's
combat stories. Here was Professor Plum's
chance to charm a certain lady, catching what he called *scarlet
fever.* "I've seen more convincing peacocking

from a tadpole," quipped Mrs. Peacock,
respectfully retiring to the library, green
tea in hand and a tickled Miss Scarlet
in tow. Mr. Boddy's absence was so brazen it bred white
noise not even tales of exemplum
heroism, narrated by and starring Colonel Mustard,

could quiet—his presence, by all accounts, as keen as mustard
and showy as a pride of peacocks.
Like a boy exiled to his room, Professor Plum
excused himself, giving the others the green
light to do the same. Mrs. White
was in the kitchen scouring skillets

when she heard who she thought was Miss Scarlet
scream. Mr. Boddy's musty
old library was a crime scene, his final fall on this white-
knuckle ride towards death. "For the dead," Mrs. Peacock
said, "the grass is greener
on the side of the living." While plumbing

Mr. Boddy's body for clues, Professor Plum
found no visible wound—the would-be host appeared scarless,
despite blood haloing his head on the shagreen
rug and a bloodstained candlestick Colonel Mustard
recognized from dinner. Mrs. Peacock
avoided the sight, turning white

as the sheet with which Mrs. White covered the corpse. Plum
sick of the "poppycock" accusations, she sped into the starlit
night in a ragtop mustang belonging to Mr. Green.

Clue

After the board game

i

"Hands down, mustard
is the tastiest condiment," coughed Professor Plum—
his full mouth feigning hunger for the greens-
only sandwiches Mrs. White
laid out for Mr. Boddy's guests. Miss Scarlet
hadn't time to peel off her peacoat

before the no-frills food, which she declined, and a pre-cocktail
cocktail, which she accepted. Colonel Mustard
refused all fare, citing the risk of sullying his scarlet
and gold Marine Corps suit, then ate the sugarplums
that happenchanced his pockets like lint. Mrs. White
funneled the motley crew into the green-

house, where Mr. Green
was rumoring—his hand bridging his mouth to Mrs. Peacock's
ear in an effort to convince the white-
haired heiress that the sandwich-making maidservant must've
poisoned their plum
wine. Mr. Boddy's award-winning scarlet

runners initially amused Miss Scarlet,
the way one is amused by another with the same name. Mr. Green
thought it odd Mr. Boddy didn't show, told Professor Plum
as much. "Here we are, pretty as peacocks,
and our host is nowhere to be found," twirling his mustache
like the villain in a silent black and white.

Minutes into the conservatory tour, Mrs. White
introduced Mr. Boddy, who lay facedown in a scarlet-
berried elder. "This man," Colonel Mustard
said, "is dead. I know death, even when it's camouflaged by greenery."
The discovery proved too much for Mrs. Peacock's
usual aplomb—

she fainted into the arms of Professor Plum.
When she came to, he appeared to her the way a white
knight would look to a distressed damsel. Semiconscious, Mrs. Peacock
pointed to the deceased's pet Scarlet
Tanager perched on a lead pipe between the body and a briefcase gushing
    green-
backs. Right away, Colonel Mustard

mustered up an alibi about admiring Mr. Boddy's plumerias.
Mr. Green followed suit with his own white-
washed version involving one Miss Scarlet and a misdemeanor plea
    copped . . .

ii
 "Dinner is served," said Mrs. White,
inviting Mr. Boddy's guests by their *noms de plume*
into the dining room for a precooked
reheated repast. Miss Scarlet
passed the pickings, which didn't pass muster,
to a rather ravenous Mr. Green.

Nobody faked affability better than Mr. Green,
waving his napkin like a white
flag, acting out the conquered in Colonel Mustard's
combat stories. Here was Professor Plum's
chance to charm a certain lady, catching what he called *scarlet*
fever. "I've seen more convincing peacocking

from a tadpole," quipped Mrs. Peacock,
respectfully retiring to the library, green
tea in hand and a tickled Miss Scarlet
in tow. Mr. Boddy's absence was so brazen it bred white
noise not even tales of exemplum
heroism, narrated by and **starring** Colonel Mustard,

could quiet——his presence, by all accounts, as keen as mustard
and showy as a pride of peacocks.
Like **a boy** exiled to his room, Professor Plum
excused himself, giving the others the green
light to do the same. Mrs. White
was in the kitchen scouring skillets

when she heard **who** she thought was Miss Scarlet
scream. Mr. Boddy's musty
old library was a crime scene, **his final** fall on this white-
knuckle ride towards death. "For the dead," Mrs. Peacock
said, "the grass is greener
on the side of the living." While plumbing

Mr. Boddy's body for clues, Professor Plum
found no visible wound——the would-be host appeared scarless,
despite blood haloing his head on the shagreen
rug and a bloodstained candlestick Colonel Mustard
recognized from dinner. Mrs. Peacock
avoided the sight, turning white

as the sheet with which Mrs. White covered the corpse. Plum
sick of the "poppycock" accusations, she sped into the starlit
night in a ragtop mustang belonging to Mr. Green.

Imagine Sisyphus Happy

Give me tonight to be inconsolable,
    so the death drive does not declare

itself, so the moonlight does not convince
    sunrise. I was born before sunrise—

when morning masquerades as night,
    the temperature of blood, quivering

mouth in mourning. How do we
    author our gentle birth, the height

we were—were we gods rolling stars across
    a sundog sky, the same as scarabs?

We fall somewhere between god
    and mineral, angel and animal,

expecting a thing as sacred as the sun to rise
    and fall like an ordinary beast.

Deer sniff lifeless fawn before leaving,
    elephants encircle the skulls and tusks

of their dead—none wanting to leave
    the bones behind, none knowing

their leave will lessen the loss. But birds
    pluck their own feathers, dogs

lick themselves to wound. Allow me this
    luxury. Give me tonight to cut

and salt the open. Give me a shovel
    to uproot the mandrake and listen

for its scream. Give me a face that toils
    so closely with stone, it is itself

stone. I promise to enter the flesh again.
    I promise to circle to ascend.

I promise to be happy tomorrow.

Even the Gods

Even the gods misuse the unfolding blue. Even the gods misread
the windflower's nod toward sunlight as consent to consume. Still,
you envy the horse that draws their chariot. Bone of their bone.
The wilting mash of air alone keeps you from scaling Olympus
with gifts of dead or dying things dangling from your mouth—
your breath, like the sea, inching away. It is rumored gods grow
where the blood of a hanged man drips. You insist on being this
man. The gods abuse your grace. Still, you'd rather live among
the clear, cloudless white, enjoying what is left of their ambrosia.
Who should be happy this time? Who brings cake to whom?
Pray the gods do not misquote your covetous pulse for chaos,
the black from which they were conceived. Even the eyes of gods
must adjust to light. Even gods have gods.

Legendary

> I don't want to end up an old drag queen.
>
> —OCTAVIA SAINT LAURENT

This is no primrose path, a life lived out
of boredom, a role played on occasion.
Category is fem-realness—devout
in the practice of pulling a fast one
on the eye. Octavia, eighth wonder . . .
I wonder, am I as legendary
as legend lets on? Only amateurs
are moved by monikers on a marquee.
Only amateurs imagine Harlem
leads to Hollywood. I can't afford such
idle delusions. So close I see them
flickering, but not close enough to touch.
So beautiful I almost forget, were
it not for history, to know better.

In Igboland

After plagues of red locusts
are unleashed by a jealous god
hell-bent on making a scene,
her way of saying *hello* or *how dare you*,
townspeople build her a mansion
of dirt, embedded with bone china,
decorated wall-to-wall with statues
made from clay farmed from anthills—
statues of tailors on their knees
hemming the pant legs of gods;
statues of diviners reading
sun-dried entrails cast onto cloths
made of cowhide; statues of babies
breaching, their mothers' legs spread
wide toward the sky, as if in praise.
Sacrifices of goats and roosters
signal headway behind the fence
that hides the construction. A day is set.
Next spirit workers disrobe and race
to the fence, which they level, heap
into piles, and set ablaze, so the offering
is first seen by firelight, not unlike
a beloved's face over candlelight.
The West in me wants the mansion
to last. The African knows it cannot.
Everything aspires to one
degradation or another. I want
to learn how to make something
holy, then walk away.

Notes

"The First Person Who Will Live to Be One Hundred and Fifty Years Old Has Already Been Born": The title is borrowed from "Who wants to live forever? Scientist sees aging cured," the Reuters article by health and science correspondent Kate Kelland.

"Candelabra with Heads": 2006, Thomas Hirschhorn, part of the Tate Collection.

"Virginia is for Lovers": The poem shares its title with the tourism and travel slogan of the Commonwealth of Virginia.

"Legendary" (Venus Xtravaganza): Venus Xtravaganza was an Italian American transgender performer featured in *Paris Is Burning*, a documentary film about drag pageants in 1980s Harlem.

"And": The poem is inspired by Thomas Sayers Ellis's poem entitled "Or," published in the October 2006 issue of *Poetry*.

"Clue": The poem is inspired by the murder mystery game, created by Anthony E. Pratt from Birmingham, England, and currently published by the U.S. company Hasbro.

"Imagine Sisyphus Happy": The title is borrowed from the final sentence of Albert Camus's essay "The Myth of Sisyphus." The lines "Give me a face that toils / so closely with stone, it is itself / stone" are also borrowed from the essay.

"Legendary" (Octavia Saint Laurent): Octavia Saint Laurent was an African American transgender performer featured in *Paris Is Burning*, a documentary film about drag pageants in 1980s Harlem.

"In Igboland": The poem refers to the construction of what is known as an *mbari* in the Owerri region of Nigeria. An *mbari* is a building erected in response to a major catastrophe and dedicated to one or several local deities. The majority of them are made for Ala, goddess of the earth.

Nicole Sealey was born in St. Thomas, U.S.V.I., and raised in Apopka, Florida. Sealey is a Cave Canem graduate fellow as well as the recipient of a 2014 Elizabeth George Foundation Grant. Her other honors include the 2014 Stanley Kunitz Memorial Prize from *The American Poetry Review*, a 2013 Daniel Varoujan Award, and the 2012 Poetry International Prize. Her work has appeared in *Best New Poets 2011*, *Harvard Review*, *Ploughshares*, *Third Coast*, and elsewhere.